J 640 Joh
Johnson, J. Angelique
The eco-neighbor's guide to
a green community

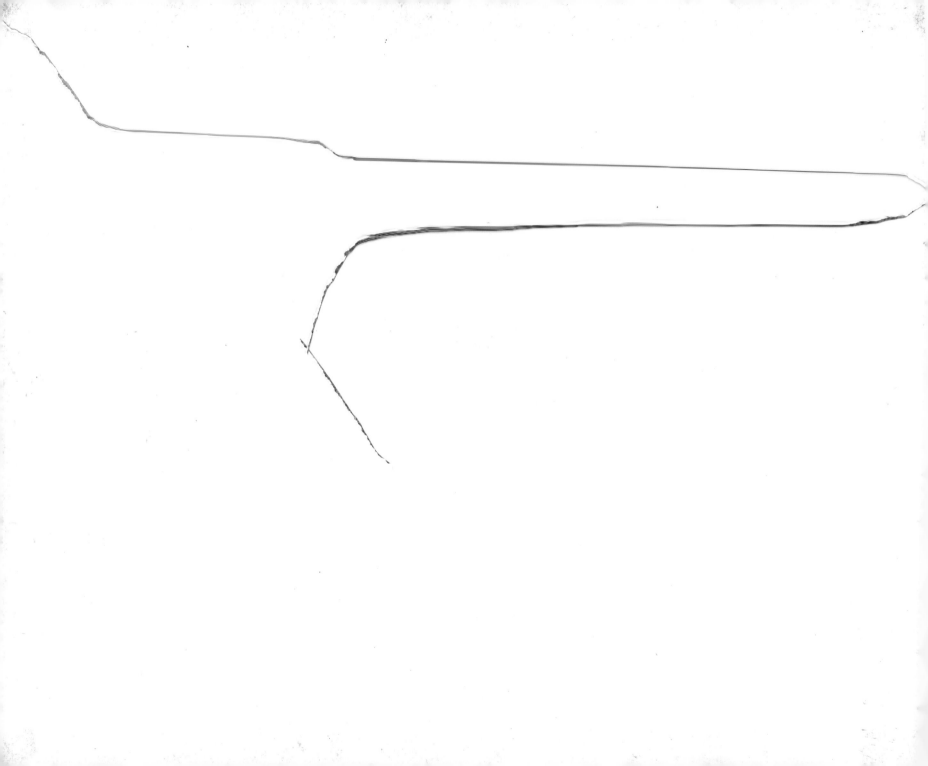

Point It Out!
TIPS FOR GREEN LIVING

Donate

The Eco-Neighbor's Guide to a

GReen Community

by J. Angelique Johnson

illustrated by Kyle Poling

PICTURE WINDOW BOOKS
a capstone imprint

It seems everyone is "going green." But do you know what living green really means? It means finding ways to keep our surroundings clean and healthy. These places include our world, communities, schools, and homes. Living green also means making healthful choices for our bodies and the bodies of others.

Look closely at each part of the community on the pages throughout this book. And check out ways you can be an eco-neighbor.

Oh, No!

Ask adults not to use harsh chemicals to fertilize the lawn. The chemicals can be harmful to humans and animals. And they can pollute waterways. Instead, choose organic fertilizers.

Oh, No!

Plastic bags sit in landfills and keep grass clippings from breaking down naturally. Instead of bagging grass clippings, use them for compost.

Did You Know...

MOWING THE LAWN WITH A GAS-POWERED LAWN MOWER CREATES MORE POLLUTION IN ONE AFTERNOON THAN 11 CARS ROARING DOWN THE HIGHWAY.

5

Way to Go!

Make recycling easy. Talk to teachers about placing recycling bins on school grounds. These bins make recycling a simple choice.

Way to Go!

Talk to teachers about planting a garden on school grounds. You'll be able to grow your own food. And you'll save the resources that would normally be used to get that same food to you.

Way to Go!

A great way to protect Earth is to plant trees. They help keep our air clean. Trees can also provide shade for buildings, keeping energy use low.

Way to Go!

By asking people to turn off their cars while waiting, you help reduce emissions.

Oh, No!

Don't serve food with lots of packaging. Food wrappers and containers add to the amount of trash going into landfills. Instead, choose foods with little packaging.

Oh, No!

Don't use plastic plates and cups. Plastic takes a long time to break down in landfills. Instead, use plates, cups, and silverware from home. And use cloth napkins. They can be washed and reused.

Oh, No!
Don't throw away that bottle! Most plastics won't break down in landfills. Throw plastic or glass bottles into a recycling bin.
Way to Go!
Check out books from the library, rather than buying books for a single read. By sharing books with others, you are saving resources.
LIBRARY
Checkout
Recycle
Donate
Oh, No!
Don't throw away old magazines or books. Take them to your library and exchange them, or place them in a recycling bin.
Way to Go!
Reuse or recycle unwanted CDs and DVDs by taking them to your local library. Millions of CDs and DVDs are thrown away each year. And they sit in landfills for many years.

Way to Go!

Stay up-to-date on the best ways to keep Earth clean. Use your local library to find books, magazines, and online resources on the subject.

Oh, No!

Don't drink or eat near library books. Take good care of library books so others can read them too.

Did You Know...

EACH YEAR, MILLIONS OF TONS OF ELECTRONICS, SUCH AS CELL PHONES AND TVS, ARE TOSSED INTO LANDFILLS. CALL YOUR LOCAL RECYCLING OR HAZARDOUS WASTE OFFICES FOR INFORMATION ABOUT WHERE TO RECYCLE THESE ITEMS.

Oh, No!

Don't let this neighborhood get run-down. Reduce waste and save resources by finding run-down parts of your community. Then, work together to clean them up.

Way to Go!

Volunteer to clean up trash along roadways. It will keep animals from eating the trash. It's also a great way to spend time with people in your community.

Living green means knowing about our natural resources. Some resources, such as wind power, are renewable. That means they most likely will never go away, no matter how much of them we use. Other resources, such as oil, can run out. We must make smart choices about how we use our natural resources. And we should be careful how much of these resources we use.

By being an eco-neighbor, you can protect Earth's resources. You can help make your community and our Earth healthy places to live. Take a look around your community. How can you make it "green?"

Glossary

bacteria—very tiny germs

chemical—a substance that creates a reaction

compost—a mixture of dead leaves, grass clippings, and even kitchen scraps that are mixed together to make fertilizer

efficient—not being wasteful

emissions—gases released into the air, often poisonous

environment—everything surrounding people, animals, and plants

evaporate—to change from a liquid into a gas

fertilizer—a substance added to soil to make plants grow better

habitat—the natural place and conditions in which a plant or animal lives

landfill—a place where garbage is dumped and buried

mulch—a layer of sawdust, paper, or dead plants spread on soil to condition it

organic—grown without the use of chemicals

pollute—to make dirty; garbage and chemicals pollute air, water, and soil

pollution—harmful materials that damage the air, water, and soil

resources—things that can be used to keep other things or people functioning; wind, sunlight, soil, and water are all examples of resources

smog—a mixture of fog and smoke that hangs in the air over cities

waterway—a place where water travels, such as rivers, streams, or canals

To Learn More

More Books to Read

Fridell, Ron. *Protecting Earth's Water Supply*. Saving Our Living Earth. Minneapolis: Lerner Publications Co., 2009.

Hock, Peggy. *Our Earth: Keeping It Clean*. Scholastic News Nonfiction Readers. New York: Children's Press, 2009.

Sirrine, Carol. *Cool Crafts with Old Wrappers, Cans, and Bottles: Green Projects for Resourceful Kids*. Green Crafts. Mankato, Minn.: Capstone Press, 2010.

Internet Sites

FactHound offers a safe, fun way to find Internet sites related to this book. All of the sites on FactHound have been researched by our staff.

Here's all you do:
Visit *www.facthound.com*
Type in this code: 9781404860285

Index

Look for all of the books in the Point It Out! Tips for Green Living series:

The Eco-Family's Guide to Living Green
The Eco-Neighbor's Guide to a Green Community
The Eco-Shopper's Guide to Buying Green
The Eco-Student's Guide to Being Green at School

Special thanks to our advisers for their expertise:

Rebecca Meyer, Extension Educator
4-H Youth Development
University of Minnesota Extension, Cloquet

Terry Flaherty, PhD, Professor of English
Minnesota State University, Mankato

Editor: Shelly Lyons
Designer: Alison Thiele
Art Director: Nathan Gassman
Production Specialist: Jane Klenk

The illustrations in this book were created digitally.
Photo Credit: Shutterstock/Doodle, 22

Picture Window Books
151 Good Counsel Drive
P.O. Box 669
Mankato, MN 56002-0669
877-845-8392
www.capstonepub.com

Printed in the United States of America, North Mankato,
Minnesota. 032010 005740CGF10

 All books published by Picture Window Books
are manufactured with paper containing at least
10 percent post-consumer waste.

Library of Congress Cataloging-in-Publication Data
Johnson, J. Angelique.
The eco-neighbor's guide to a green community /
by J. Angelique Johnson, illustrated by Kyle Poling.
p. cm. — (Point it out! tips for green living)
Includes index.
ISBN 978-1-4048-6028-5 (library binding)
1. Sustainable living—Juvenile literature. 2. Green
movement—Juvenile literature. 3. Community life—Juvenile
literature.
I. Poling, Kyle. II. Title.
GE196.J66 2011
640—dc22   2010009883